HANNAH'S GIFT

Family Restoration

Hannah's Gift: Family Restoration
Dr. Kristi Miller

1 East Bode Road
Streamwood, IL 60107-6658 U.S.A.
awana.org
(630) 213-2000

2   3   4   5   6   19   18   17   16   15

HANNAH'S GIFT

Family Restoration

Dr. Kristi Miller

contents

lesson **1** *summary*

JEREMIAH'S WORLD — INTRODUCTION

Jeremiah labored tirelessly in the hope that he could lead his people out of their messed up thinking and back to a healthy standing with the Lord and each other. He encouraged the people to use their time of captivity to prepare themselves for the day when they would be restored to their land and their people.

APPLICATION

Now that incarcerated moms have established the importance of ongoing involvement in the lives of their children, they must take steps to prepare themselves to build healthy family structures upon release. We want to use Jeremiah's words and warnings as signposts to lead us along the journey to healthy relationships.

lesson

1

INTRODUCTION

memory verse

I press on toward the goal for the prize of the upward call of God in Christ Jesus. (Philippians 3:14)

day 1   ## HANNAH'S GIFT REVIEW

In the *Hannah's Gift: The Heart of a Mother* study, we established the continued role of the mother in the life of her child even during incarceration. Though you may be separated from your child, you can still strive to leave a spiritual legacy, just as was modeled through Hannah and her son, Samuel. Each week, continue to declare the Hannah's Gift Pledge as a reminder of the commitment to God's ongoing work in your life.

HANNAH'S GIFT PLEDGE

> As a Hannah's Gift mom, I acknowledge that my children are a gift from God. I take hold of the call and responsibility as a mother and I seek God's guidance on how to best parent my child. I am growing into a wise and strong woman of faith, and my greatest desire is to leave behind a spiritual legacy carried on by my children to their children. May my family prove to be a tower of strength built on the firm foundation I am laying in the power of Christ.

As we hang on to what we have learned in *Hannah's Gift: The Heart of a Mother*, we press forward on our journey. As we look both to the present and the future, we ask: "What can I do now to prepare myself to be reunited with my child/family?"

Please do not be deceived; a perfect life, free of all problems and difficulties, is not beyond those gates and steel bars. Family life is hard. Parenting is hard. Surviving in this world is hard.

Are you ever tempted to think: If only _____, then I could really be happy! In what ways have you filled in that blank?

What have you mistakenly believed would fix your problems?

Just as we take hold of our responsibility as mothers, now we take hold of our responsibility to do what is in our power to create a healthy family life. God wants to restore our families.

Are you ready to roll up your sleeves and get to work? We are going to use the prophet Jeremiah as a model. As with Hannah's world, Jeremiah's world was in a major mess. While some of his people had been taken into captivity, the others were dealing with a soon-coming war with the Babylonians. In addition, false prophets were misleading the people by telling them no harm would come to them.

FALSE WORSHIP

To get a good feel of his situation, read Jeremiah 7:21-28. Basically, Jeremiah was told up front that the people would not listen to him. In this passage, what indicates God's patience and long-suffering toward His people before He finally acts in judgment?

The first part of this passage lets us know that the people of Judah continued to obey the written law. In other words, they still went to worship services, offered sacrifices, and did as the priests told them. They thought that just because they were going through the motions of religious practices, God would be happy with them. However, God said they were stiff-necked and stubborn. The term *stiff-necked* is a plowing term. It refers to cattle that refuse to let their master put a yoke on them. The animal stiffens his neck in stubbornness, so as to fight against his master's will. In other words, the people were always fighting against God.

Additionally, God's people added other pagan worship activities to their Yahweh (God's special covenant name) worship, showing that their hearts were far from recognizing the one true God. Read further in Jeremiah 7:30-31. Write some of the shocking additional worship activities.

assignment ....

Evaluate your own life for any areas of stubbornness and false worship.

day 2   **FALSE SECURITIES**

In the midst of the disorder, false prophets proclaimed that God would not let Babylon destroy them or the sacred temple. Read what God has to say about that in the first part of Chapter 7 (verses 1-8). What do you think are the deceptive words mentioned in verse 8?

If you don't know the answer, verses 12-15 give a clue. The place of Shiloh is where the tabernacle of the Lord once stood. Jeremiah tells the people that if they don't think God will let His sacred place be destroyed, then just go visit Shiloh. In other words, the tabernacle fell to ruin at Shiloh, and the temple is about the fall to ruin by the Babylonian army.

The temple provided the people a false sense of security. What have you mistakenly taken as your source of safety? Have you looked to money for a sense of security? Have drugs or has alcohol been a false means of protection? Perhaps you have used a hardened and calloused exterior to make you feel safe. Like the Israelites, have you used religious practices as your safety? Be brave enough to ask God to tear down anything you use to hide behind. Be open before God and others. You may feel helpless for a while, but eventually you will learn to trust God as your mighty fortress, a security that cannot be shaken!

assignment ·

Write out any false securities in your life. Describe what needs to happen to exchange false security for true security in God.

day 3   **FALSE MESSAGES OF HOPE**

The false prophets lied to the people by telling them to run to the temple for safety. For another explanation of these false prophets, read Jeremiah 14:13-16. Write down the specifics of the message of the false prophets. What were these false prophets saying?

It's dangerous business to listen to false prophets! Describe what will become of those who believed the lies of those prophets.

Another lie the false prophets proclaimed concerned the people that already had been taken captive in the first waves of war with the Babylonians. The false prophets told the people to expect God's quick and speedy release of the captives. Jeremiah counters this teaching with a comparison (metaphor) about two baskets of figs. Read Jeremiah 24:1-10 and answer the questions below.

The basket of good figs represents what group of people?

The basket of bad figs represents what group of people?

What promises are made to the good figs?

What would be the outcome of the bad figs?

Contrary to the messages of the false prophets, Jeremiah proclaimed it better to be taken into exile than to remain in the land. The remnant of God's people, the ones through whom God would rebuild His people, would come from those in exile (captivity).

assignment

Reflect on how the basket of figs metaphor might apply to your life.

day 1   FALSE REALITY

Many parallels can be made from Jeremiah's world to the world of an incarcerated person. It was not God's intention for His people to turn away from Him and worship idols with all sorts of evil practices. However, the ones taken away are going to be the ones rescued. Perhaps you have family members and friends on the outside who think they are better off because they are free, but still continue to be blinded to the dangers of their own life choices. Do you know of those who have adopted a false sense of security that prohibits them from truly facing reality?

Could it be that God will build a remnant through you, the one taken into captivity?

Jeremiah has some serious lessons to teach us. He uses strong language, so brace yourself. Jeremiah will be in your face at times. His point to his people in Judah is this: You are about to be taken into captivity because of rebellion toward God, but your captivity can be valuable so don't waste it. If you will turn to the Lord, you will be restored from your captivity to a greater peace and security (Jeremiah 33:1-13).

The prophecies of Jeremiah during his great time of turmoil are still profitable to us today. We will use Jeremiah's messages to determine principles for healthy families. Jeremiah labored tirelessly in the hope that he could lead his people out of their messed up thinking and back to a healthy standing with the Lord and each other. In the same way, we want to use Jeremiah's words and warnings as signposts to lead us to healthy relationships.

 *assignment*

Write down your first response to Jeremiah's message, which stated that the ones taken in captivity would be better off than the ones not taken.

day 5   AVOIDING A FALSE START

Reading in the Old Testament, especially the Old Testament prophets, can be overwhelming. To make sure we have a clear understanding of the principles, today's lesson will encourage you to review the elements of Jeremiah's story covered so far.

Jeremiah's land was called Judah. What country (or people group) was Judah in battle with during Jeremiah's ministry?

Though the people of Judah were very religious and seemed to worship God actively, what kinds of false worship did they practice?

How did the temple give the people a false sense of security?

What did the basket of figs represent?

assignment ....

Take a moment to review the answers you gave to the daily assignments. Reflect on your thoughts and attitude about your incarceration. Write down any fears or concerns you have about doing this 10-week Bible study.

Review your memory verse — Philippians 3:14. See if you can write it below from memory.

lesson 2 summary

JEREMIAH'S WORLD — CAPTIVITY

The prophet Jeremiah wrote letters to those who had already been taken into Babylonian captivity. His message to them was to stop fighting against God and stop putting their hopes in a quick rescue. The captivity was of God and they had something to gain from it.

APPLICATION

The degree of your restoration is going to be dependent on what you learn during your captive years. Don't waste this time! Now is the chance to learn and practice healthy relationship skills that will strengthen your relationships with your children and other family members.

lesson

2

THE YEARS OF CAPTIVITY

---

memory verse

"For I know the plans I have for you," declares the LORD, "plans for welfare and not for evil, to give you a future and a hope." (Jeremiah 29:11)

day 1   GOD'S PLANS

"For I know the plans I have for you," declares the LORD, "plans
for welfare and not for evil, to give you a future and a hope."
(Jeremiah 29:11)

As a correctional minister, I use some form of Jeremiah 29:11
almost daily. In the prison setting, I deal with broken individuals
who feel discarded by society. Many of them are buckling under
the weight of their own guilt and can't see past their regrets and
consequences. Could there be any sweeter words for such persons
than to hear that God still has a purpose for their lives? They
need to know that He is not done with them and has not discarded them no matter what. It's not over, and all is not lost. There is
always hope of redemption!

What about you? Have you claimed this promise for yourself?
Have you shared it with others as a word of encouragement?
If so, write about it below.

As wonderful as this good news is, we must be careful not to take
it out of context and bypass what the Word is really speaking.
We need to be confident when we speak the promise of Jeremiah
29:11 that we do so in the spirit in which it was intended.

assignment  . . . .

To ensure proper interpretation of this passage, read the entire
chapter of Jeremiah 29. Tomorrow we will look at the context
and the original audience to which it was given.

day 2   JEREMIAH'S WORLD

By the time of the prophet Jeremiah's day, God's people long had been in stubborn rebellion. They had mistakenly believed that God would not call them out because they were His chosen people. While the nation of Babylon breathed down their necks, the people of Judah falsely put their hope in the presence of the temple, believing that God would never let anything happen to His sacred location (Jeremiah 7:1-15). And while the prophet Jeremiah proclaimed the soon-coming destruction of the temple and Jerusalem around it, false prophets gave the misleading hope of God's protection without any conditions.

Read the first chapter of Jeremiah. Write down any phrases of reassurance that God gives to Jeremiah.

God encouraged Jeremiah a great deal because the ministry intended for him was so heavy. Read the message Jeremiah is called to deliver to his own people in Jeremiah 1:14-16. The north represents the strong and scary Babylonian army. Below, summarize what Jeremiah is to preach.

It may go without saying that Jeremiah was not a popular prophet. Everyone, even his own family, hated him for his messages of judgment and defeat of their nation at the hands of the Babylonians. They much preferred the false prophets' message that God would rescue them and deliver them from their enemies. Jeremiah didn't enjoy being the bearer of bad news. He actually despised his assignment from the Lord (Jeremiah 20:7-18). But no matter how hard it got, Jeremiah remained faithful. We have a faithful God who does not leave or forsake us. He is calling us to reflect His faithfulness to our families. Our job as parents is not easy. Are you willing to be faithful and obedient, trusting that God will fight for you and be with you and rescue you (Jeremiah 1:19)?

assignment ·

Describe how important it was for Jeremiah to speak and live the truth even when it would cause him hardship. Evaluate whether or not you have that same attitude about parenthood.

day 3 THE PROMISE'S IMPACT

Though Jeremiah's ministry was to those living in Jerusalem, a portion of his people had already been taken into exile to Babylon as captives (Jeremiah 1:3). At some point, Jeremiah writes a letter to those living in Babylon. Read the contents of this letter now in Jeremiah 29:1-23.

You should have noticed that Jeremiah tells the captives to marry, buy houses, plant gardens, and basically settle into life in Babylon. Remember, Babylon represents the enemy of God to them. False prophets were telling the people in exile that God would soon deliver them out of their enemy's hand. Jeremiah says just the opposite. He even tells them to pray for the prosperity of

Babylon! How appalling that must have been to the captives! It is in the context of this letter that the 29:11 promise is given. In other words, Jeremiah is telling the exiles to settle in and make the most of life in captivity, but he also includes the fact that the captivity will not last forever. As a matter of fact, it will last for 70 years, at which time God would bring His people back to the land and restore them. Why? Because He had a plan to prosper them and give them a future. Notice the corresponding nature of the promise. The conclusion is that the time in captivity would lead them to turn and seek God. When they do, He will be found by them. The time of captivity was a consequence of their rebellion, but it didn't mean that God was done with them. Yes, there is hope even in captivity that God can bring you back no matter how far you've wandered.

CONTEXT OF THE INCARCERATED WORLD

Just as with those of Jeremiah's day, sometimes it takes a drastic prison sentence to finally get a person to respond to God. At the moment, we want to cry out, "Why, God?". But deep down, we know why. We know that a long line of rebellion came before the time of incarceration.

Jeremiah explained that the exile called for a turning back to the Lord. In the same way, the prison sentence sits a person down so that he or she can hear from God, submit to His plan, and enjoy His blessings even while in captivity.

In what ways can you relate your prison sentence with the time of captivity described by Jeremiah?

Take a moment and sketch a timeline of major events in your life leading up to your incarceration. Note particularly when you sensed God's voice urging you to turn to Him.

day 1   OUR SITUATION'S POTENTIAL

If we use the Jeremiah 29:11 promise as a blanket statement to everyone, we have misused the Scripture. This promise was specifically for God's people living in Judah. Is there a universal and timeless truth? Yes, but to whom and in what circumstance? Those who seek the Lord with all sincerity. A person who has turned to the Lord and away from their sin can have great assurance that God has a plan and purpose for them, and will use their captivity as a means to draw them close to Himself. The first part of 29:11 states: *For I* [the Lord] *know the plans I have for you.* The only way we can know them, then, is to seek Him. If a person is not interested in seeking the Lord, they forfeit the right to know the hope and future that would be available to them.

Read the context of the promise: Jeremiah 29:10-14. Write down the actions of God and the actions of the people.

Actions of God	Actions of the People

If a person is truly looking up, looking to be in fellowship with God, to repent and turn to God, then by all means let's share the Jeremiah 29:11 promise. The larger context of the passage teaches that though we must bear the consequences for our actions, we do not lose hope. Just as with Jeremiah's audience, God can use the valley of our bad decisions and actions to make us stronger and bring us out of captivity conformed more to His image than previously would have been possible.

Make a comparison between your situation and that of the nation of Judah.

God's People in Judah	You

Sentence: 70 years

Place of exile: Babylon

Disobedience: Worship of foreign gods

The remainder of this study will be based on your commitment to settle in, live at peace where you are, and use this time to turn back to the Lord. Remember, He wants to restore you after and even during your time of captivity. The degree of your restoration is going to be dependent on what you learn during these down years. You can continue to fight against your circumstances, even put your hope in a quick delivery. But neither will bring about the transformation God has planned for you. Don't waste this time. Jeremiah's message to the exiles is that they are going to be better off than those not taken into exile. In other words, the free people of Jerusalem end up dying because of their own sin. The exiles, the ones taken into captivity, actually have a chance to get things right and be restored back to God. What a contradiction!

Are you willing to settle in to your time of captivity? Will you let God use this time to transform you into something beautiful and useful to Him and to your family? How would this look in your facility?

assignment ....

Write down specific ways you can make wise use of your time of captivity to grow and move forward.

day 5   THE PROMISE'S REVIEW

To make sure we have a clear understanding of the message, today's lesson will encourage you to review the information covered in Jeremiah 29.

Where was Jeremiah when he wrote the letter to the exiles?

What is another name for exile?

Where were the exiles living?

What false message of hope were the false prophets giving the exiles?

The people didn't want Jeremiah's message. They hated the message and the messenger. Perhaps you are less than excited to begin to see your incarceration in a positive light.

assignment . . . .

Are you willing, though, to give the message a chance? Write down your thoughts below.

Review your memory verse — Jeremiah 29:11. See if you can write it below from memory.

HANNAH'S GIFT PLEDGE

As a **Hannah's Gift** *mom, I acknowledge that my children are a gift from God. I take hold of the call and responsibility as a mother and I seek God's guidance on how to best parent my child. I am growing into a wise and strong woman of faith, and my greatest desire is to leave behind a spiritual legacy carried on by my children to their children. May my family prove to be a tower of strength built on the firm foundation I am laying in the power of Christ.*

lesson 3 *summary*

JEREMIAH'S WORLD —
SETTLING IN: COMMUNICATION

Jeremiah told the people in captivity to settle down into life in Babylon and ... *seek the welfare of the city* ... *(Jeremiah 29:7)*. During this time, they are instructed to seek the Lord, to go to Him and pray to Him, and He will be found by them.

APPLICATION

The time of incarceration should be used to seek the Lord and learn His ways. This lesson will demonstrate how to use the prison setting to learn good communication skills that will be helpful during and after incarceration. Healthy communication is an important key to healthy families.

lesson

3

SETTLING IN:
HEALTHY COMMUNICATION

---

memory verse

Let no corrupting talk come out of your mouths, but only such as is good for building up, as fits the occasion, that it may give grace to those who hear. (Ephesians 4:29)

day 1 COMMUNICATION OPPORTUNITIES

Once again read the letter Jeremiah wrote to those in captivity in Jeremiah 29:1-23. In what ways can you use what you have where you are? Write down opportunities that are available to you today that you know would help you to thrive and succeed in life.

How can you take advantage of spiritual growth opportunities right now? In what ways does the incarcerated setting benefit spiritual growth? What barriers exist in the free world that are now removed in prison?

As we actively pursue our relationship with God, we want to work on our relationship with others. Luke 2:52 says: *And Jesus increased in wisdom and in stature and in favor with God and man.* We too want to develop mentally, physically, and progress in how we relate to God and others.

God has wired women to be in relationships. Our hearts are bent toward family. My work in a women's prison has really proved this point more than any psychology text could have. There is a practice in my prison that seems to happen naturally: the creation of play families. The terms *play momma* and *play child* are common vocabulary in my setting. Since they are separated from their own families, the women tend to gravitate toward creating prison families of their own. Often these play families produce unhealthy codependences and other types of abuses, so I generally don't encourage this practice. However, if washed in the Word, inmates can utilize this concept to practice healthy relationships for their outside families. In line with the settling in theme, I am proposing that you begin practicing how to build a healthy family with those you see as family within the prison population. Later in the lesson we will define the biblical concept of family and look at each member's role. For now, however, let's begin with something more basic: communication tips. Whether you want to or not, you must interact with others in your institution every day: your roommate, the guards, people classified in the same work area, etc. The communication tips covered in this lesson are not only beneficial to healthy families, but they work to create healthy relationships everywhere and in every case. Tomorrow we will begin to discover what the Bible has to say about healthy communication.

assignment ....

Poll a few people you live around. Ask them to give you feedback on your communication skills. Don't get angry if their answers aren't what you hoped for!

day 2   COMMUNICATION QUESTIONS

Read Ephesians 4:29. In this one verse we learn important basic communication practices. We need to train ourselves to filter everything that pops into our mind through this verse before we let it out of our mouth! Before you speak, ask yourself:

1. Is it necessary? Certainly, if your words are going to be corrupting, then they are unnecessary! Think about it. Does what you are about to say really need to be said?

    a. Continue to read in Ephesians 5:3-4. What is meant by crude joking?

    b. Perhaps you have accepted obscene conversation as just part of the prison culture. But what does God's Word say? If you truly wish to submit to God's authority, then you must put away immoral talk. Give a few examples of situations that encourage this type of language.

    c. Do you tend to bring up a subject just to draw attention to yourself? Read Proverbs 27:2. Who should do the bragging about you? Test yourself. Engage in conversation with a few people today and notice how many times you want to turn the talk toward or about yourself. Record your experience below.

    d. A good principle to live by is this: When in doubt, shut your mouth. See Proverbs 10:19. Sometimes the smartest thing we can do is to keep quiet!

2. Is it true? Read Proverbs 26:28.

    a. Sometimes we use empty words to flatter others in an attempt to manipulate the person or situation. Sometimes we just flat out lie about others to make us feel better about ourselves. Are you tempted to spread a piece of gossip about someone that may not be true? Be ready to share an example (leave out specific names!).

    b. Even if the gossip is true, by spreading it, you are defaming that person's character. In doing so, what part of Ephesians 4:29 have you violated?

3. Is it beneficial to building up others? While we do not want to give false flattery, we do want to take every opportunity to use our words to build up others. Read Proverbs 16:24. What effect do gracious or pleasant words have on a person?

assignment ....

Ephesians 4:29 is your memory verse for this week. Assess how well you live out this verse from day-to-day.

day 3 COMMUNICATION GUIDELINES

Our tongues hold the power of life and death. Think about how the words of others have affected you. As a mother, you want to choose your words toward your children carefully. Harshness and criticism is contagious in families. If this was how you were brought up, you will need to be deprogrammed in how you talk to others. Share below the communication style modeled to you in your family.

The truth of the matter is that we talk more harshly to those we love. We feel that they love and accept us. Therefore, we don't have to be so careful not to hurt their feelings or offend them. Nothing could be further from the truth. Our words to them carry even greater power to build up or tear down, so be on guard! Ask God to show you when you speak harshly to those you love.

We need to return to the old motherly advice with our children: "If you don't have anything nice to say, don't say anything at all!" But let's also be sure to practice what we preach!

assignment ....

Evaluate the next phone call home. Reflect on your latest conversations with your friends and prison family. Do you tend to speak more sharply with those closest to you?

day 4 COMMUNICATION RESPONSES

Read the following verses and summarize the main point of each.

James 1:19-20:

Psalm 141:3-4:

James 3:9-10:

assignment . . . .

**Write how you will respond to what the Bible says about the
tongue.**

day 5   COMMUNICATION CHALLENGE

I estimate that about 95 percent of the problems in my prison would be resolved if we all could keep our mouths shut! I am referring to inmates, security, administration, and everyone in between. There is a reason God gave us two ears and one mouth. We should listen twice as much as we speak. Sadly, we have it the other way around.

assignment ....

Read Proverbs 10:19 once again. Reflect over the past 24 hours. Write down any words that hurt you or affected you negatively in any way. Now write down any way your own words may have caused someone else harm or pain.

Silence Challenge: Choose a four-hour block of time (not in the middle of sleeping hours!) and practice complete silence. Instead of talking, listen closely to the conversations of others all around you. Record your observations below.

Review your memory verse for this week — Ephesians 4:29. See if you can write it below from memory.

lesson 4 summary

JEREMIAH'S WORLD — SETTLING IN: AUTHORITY

Jeremiah told the people in captivity to settle down into life in Babylon and … *seek the welfare of the city* … They are told specifically to submit to the authority of the wicked Babylonians (Jeremiah 27:8-11). In doing so, God would honor their submission and restore them to their land.

APPLICATION

An attitude of submission is a Christian characteristic that we all must embrace and is essential in order to be a strong family.

lesson

4

SETTLING IN:
SUBMIT TO AUTHORITY

memory verse

Submitting to one another out of reverence for Christ.
(Ephesians 5:21)

day 1   GOD'S AUTHORITY

What does it mean to make Jesus the Lord of your life? You die to self. You give yourself away. He has the right to your life. We submit to His authority over us, knowing that His way for us is always what is best for us. To rebel against that authority is to run out from the protection of His wings.

We want our children to submit to our parental authority. Why? We believe we know better how to live life than our children. We have a greater understanding of how things are, and we want them to learn and grow from our wisdom. So it is with God. Read Isaiah 55:8-9 and describe how this mirrors our standing with our children.

When it comes down to it, all sin is rebellion. What is in the middle of sin? I! You say, "I will do this my way, not God's. I know better than God." By doing things my way, I rebel against His authority over me.

assignment

How do you feel about surrendering to God's authority over you? Does it stir up resentment or does it cause you to have peace?

day 2 ISRAEL'S REBELLION

Read Jeremiah 2:1-13.

How does Jeremiah describe the people's relationship with God in verses 1-3? Though they had done nothing to earn God's favor, the people of Judah were God's chosen people and blessed as His covenant people. God fought their battles and destroyed their enemies.

In verses 4-8, God lays out His case against His people. Read those verses again, and summarize the basic argument presented.

The people of Judah had rejected God's blessings and instead, responded with rebellion. He states that they followed worthlessness (false idols) and became worthless (5b). I've seen this progression so many times. Some people have had every opportunity to know God and enjoy His fellowship. They enjoyed a Christian family and loving influences that pointed them to God. Yet they rejected God's love and grace and ran after the worthless gods this world offers. It doesn't take long before they begin to reflect the worthlessness of the world's trappings and leave far behind the glory of God. Have you experienced this or seen this progression in your own life or someone else's? How do we begin to reflect the environment and attitudes we choose?

After the argument is built, then God brings charges against His people. Read verses 9-13 again. Notice the two-fold action described in verse 13. Describe the first sin.

Now describe the second sin.

Let's take a look at the comparison between a spring and a cistern. In the Judean area where Jeremiah lived, water was available in one of three forms. The first and best was living water. This type of water is fresh, such as a spring from the ground. Have you ever had water straight from a spring? It's the clearest and freshest water you have ever tasted!

The second option for water in Judea was from a well. One would dig deep into the ground to access the water table below the earth. The water could be lifted out and brought to the surface by a bucket on a rope.

The third option for water was from a cistern. A cistern was a deep, sometimes tunneling, channel dug in the ground and then plastered so that the walls and bottom of the cistern would not leak. There was and still is very little rainfall in the Judean region. The purpose of these cisterns was to catch the runoff of water whenever it did rain. These deep cisterns sometimes would be filled with years-old, stagnant rainwater that could be used for drinking and cooking. The cisterns were open for anything to fall into and rest at the bottom of the collected water. Are you thinking what I am thinking? Gross! To make matters worse, sometimes the plaster walls of the cistern would crack and then the water you worked so hard to save would seep into the earth. Now that you know the difference between springs of living water and cisterns, read verse 13 again and describe the significance of the exchange Judah has made in their rejection of God.

assignment . . . .

How have you been guilty of rejecting living water for stagnant cistern water?

Day 3 HUMAN AUTHORITY

In short, Judah rebelled against God. See Jeremiah 2:20. Though we may not be bold enough to tell God, "I will not serve You," our actions can speak louder than our words. Are you willing to be under God's authority?

If you are convinced of God's goodness and love toward you, it is likely you do not have much of a resistance to His authority. But what about man's authority over you? Is there not something in us that bucks up quickly whenever someone tries to rule over us? Everything in us tells us that we have the right to be free from all yoke of authority. But what does God say about that? Are human authority systems of God?

First, let's look at some biblical examples where God's people needed to rebel against authority. Read Daniel 3 and describe how and why the three young men rebelled against their authority. What was the outcome?

Now read Daniel 6 and describe how and why Daniel rebelled against his authority. What was the outcome?

Young David, before he became king of Israel, once served in the house of King Saul. David was a mighty man of strength and military ability, and the people quickly realized he would be a better king than Saul. Saul, of course, became very jealous of David, even to the point of wishing to kill him. David had to run for his life, but Saul pursued him relentlessly. Read 1 Samuel 24. Summarize this narrative below:

Though David had every right to kill Saul in the name of self-defense (Saul had been pursing David to kill him for quite a while), he did not do it. Why? Because he understood he still had a responsibility to respect Saul's authority as king. Notice that David did run away from Saul when he threatened his life. In other words, we are not expected to submit to authority when our life is in danger. Yet the attitude of David was still one of submission even while he fled for his safety.

assignment ·

In light of the Scripture reading for today, describe a situation in which you think it is appropriate to disregard human authority.

day 4 BIBLICAL TEACHING

Today, we will look at some biblical examples that speak positively about human authority, even when that authority is not godly.

Read Romans 13:1-7 and 1 Peter 2:13-15. Give a summary of what these verses describe.

Another biblical example of an earthy authority figure being used by God is found in Isaiah 44:28-45:3. Read that passage now and describe the crucial event Cyrus would bring about.

This describes Cyrus the Great as the Lord's servant, used by God to bring the Israelites back from their land of captivity and return them to their promised land. Cyrus, by no means, was a follower of God, yet he was still an instrument in God's hand used to bless and benefit God's people. Do you believe God can use a Cyrus in your life to bring about God's blessings to you even though they are unaware they are doing so?

When you take all of these biblical teachings on human authority together, we can summarize a few key points.

1. We are within our right to defy authority when we are asked to violate the beliefs of our faith. This was the case in Daniel, where these men were asked to participate in the worship of other gods. (For another example of this, see Acts 4.)

2. We have the approval of God to run from authority that is abusive or threatening to our lives. In doing so, we must maintain an attitude of submission even while on the run.

3. Private vengeance is forbidden; we must operate within the confines of authorized officials. These earthly rulers are servants who are answerable to the one true God.

4. Christians should never assume that loyalty to Jesus gives freedom for civil disobedience, which would only reshuffle political powers. We are to live as a sign of the kingdom yet to come, a kingdom characterized by justice, peace, and joy in the Spirit (Romans 14:17). This kingdom cannot be ushered in by violence and hatred. As Christians we are to be revolutionary, not rebellious.

Reflect on how you feel about what the Bible says about human authority.

day 5   OUR SUBMISSION

Now we are ready to talk about Jeremiah's setting. He clearly tells his people to submit to the Babylonians. Further, God makes it clear that He is using the king of Babylon to bring about His will! Read Jeremiah 27:1-15. What did Jeremiah symbolize by wearing a yoke around his neck?

Make no mistake about it; the Babylonian's authority was anything but pleasant. God's people were the captives, the slaves, of Babylon. Yet it was God's will for them to be subject to the Babylonians for a season. We must remember that God is sovereign. His reign is ultimate and far greater than human kings/rulers that will come and go. When you submit to the human authority placed over you, you are really submitting to God's supreme reign.

Bondservants, obey in everything those who are your earthly masters, not by way of eye-service, as people-pleasers, but with sincerity of heart, fearing the Lord. Whatever you do, work heartily, as for the Lord and not for men. (Colossians 3:22-23)

Simply put, submission is a Christian characteristic modeled for us by Christ Himself.

Write Ephesians 5:21 below:

Read Philippians 2:3-11 several times. What does it mean to have the mind (attitude) of Christ?

As believers, we have been given a realm of authority over the Devil, this world, and sin. But God will not bless our rebellion. I love the way Adrian Rogers said it: "… You cannot be over those things that God wants you to be over until you learn to be under those things that God has set over you."[1] Could it be that you have not been able to get victory in certain areas of your life because you are rebellious in other areas?

---

1. Adrian Rogers, *The Incredible Power of Kingdom Authority: Getting an Upper Hand on the Underworld* (Nashville, TN: B&H Publishing, 2002), p. 63.

assignment ....

Reflect and let God search your heart over the issue of submission. Look for any connection between rebellion and areas of defeat in your life.

Review your memory verse for this week — Ephesians 5:21. See if you can write it below from memory.

lesson 5 summary

JEREMIAH'S WORLD — DEEP HEALING

The prophets and priests were treating the wounds as if they were not serious by not giving the truth to the people. They told them what they wanted to hear and ignored the spiritual sickness that was leading to soon-coming death.

APPLICATION

We must be honest about the seriousness of our wounds and allow God to heal us through and through. To walk in victory and power will take more than just a Jesus bandage. We need the Great Physician to treat every sickness.

lesson

5

TREAT THE WOUNDS

memory verses

For from the least to the greatest of them, everyone is greedy for unjust gain; and from prophet to priest, everyone deals falsely. They have healed the wound of My people lightly, saying, "Peace, peace," when there is no peace.
(Jeremiah 6:13-14)

day 1   **SERIOUS WOUNDS**

As we have already seen in previous lessons, the people of Jeremiah's day would not hear his judgment message. They only wanted to hear positive prophecies. Compare this with the apostle Paul's words in 2 Timothy 4:2-4. What is Paul saying?

Even the people entrusted with God's Word withheld the life-giving truth from the people. Read Jeremiah 6:13-15. How have we seen this in our own time? In what ways have those in spiritual leadership positions kept the truth from the people?

What is the connection of greed with false messages of peace? Do you see this same connection with certain prosperity gospel preachers today?

Bible versions translate Jeremiah 6:14a in this way:

They dress the wound of My people as though it were not serious. (NIV)

They have healed the wound of My people lightly. (ESV)

They have healed also the hurt ... of My people slightly. (KJV)

They have also healed the hurt of My people slightly. (NKJV)

I spent 13 years as a registered nurse in the oncology field. I had my share of dressing wounds. We typically think of wounds resulting from accidents such as falling, being shot, being cut, etc. The wounds I dealt with the most were surgical wounds. The doctor would intentionally cut a person open for the purpose of removing the cancerous parts. This was all done in a sterile environment, so the surgical wound could be closed up with stitches or staples. Without complications, the surgical wound would heal in a week or so. Sometimes, though, bacteria would enter into the area and the surgical site would become infected. One would think that the best thing to do would be to treat the visible symptoms while leaving the internal layers protected. A good nurse knows, however, that true healing can only come by opening up the wound and getting all the way to the bottom of it. Healing must take place from the bottom up. The typical process would be to open up the wound by removing whatever was holding it together (stitches or staples) and then to pack in sterile gauze all the way to the bottom. Two to three times a day, bacteria-saturated gauze would be removed and fresh packing would be put in place. The process of healing through packing and repacking could take weeks and even months. It is painful and the gaping wound is ugly. Initially one may even think, *This looked better before we opened it up!* But to cover the area superficially would only allow the wound to abscess and rot from the inside, causing the person to become poisoned with infection, possibly leading to death.

Just like a good doctor or nurse should not ignore the signs of infection by covering over the wound, someone who follows Christ and knows the Word can't decide not to treat the wounds in his or her own life. If you are going to have healthy relationships with your family and others, you must let the Great Physician tend to your wounds. It will be ugly for a while. It will even be painful. But don't halt the process until full healing is achieved.

assignment ....

Spend time in prayer with the Great Physician. Will you trust Him to treat your wounds?

day 2 FIRST LAYER: DENIAL OF SIN

Read Jeremiah 8:4-12 to find out where we start. I will use my nursing analogy (illustration or picture) of wound healing to describe how to get to the bottom of our issues.

The very bottom level of the wound is denial of your own sin. Read 8:4-6. In what ways are you clinging to deceit? What area of your life have you refused to turn over to God?

Never underestimate your potential to self-deceive. Sometimes we are the problem and we don't even realize it! Be willing to let trustworthy people speak truth to you. Regularly expose your heart to God, asking Him to reveal to you any area of offense (Psalm 139:23-24). Don't cling to your deceit. If the Holy Spirit brings an area of conviction to you, rejoice! He is still giving you a chance to repent. Have a regular practice of repentance.

Meditate on 1 John 1:8-2:2 now. Write a summary of these verses below. What should we do as we recognize our sin?

day 3   SECOND LAYER: CONTINUING DESTRUCTIVE BEHAVIOR

The second layer of our wound is the continuation of destructive behavior.

Read Jeremiah 8:4-5. When a man falls down, doesn't he get up? In other words, logically shouldn't we expect to learn from our mistakes and not repeat them? Read Jeremiah 2:23-25. Through the comparisons of animals in heat, how does Jeremiah describe the people of Judah?

We must come to the point of realizing our own powerlessness to change our behavior. What areas of your life seem out of control right now? What behavior have you only hidden away under a bandage, as if it were not serious?

Only through walking in the Spirit can we bear fruit of righ-
teousness. Take a look at the list of the fruit of the Spirit in
Galatians 5:22-23. Which of you can force yourself to produce
one of these? Describe how you can experience these qualities in
your life.

day 4   THIRD LAYER: ABUSE OF RELATIONSHIPS

As we continue with my nursing analogy, the third layer of the
wound is the abuse of relationships. Carefully read Jeremiah
7:3-7. So far we have focused on the people's idol worship as an
offense to God. What other activities is God equally unhappy
with?

We must be honest about the way we have used people as a means
to satisfy our own wounded hearts. Whom have you set up to be
your "savior"? This would be the one you look to for fulfillment
and purpose. Guess what? They will let you down. They were
never meant to be your source of happiness.

Whom have you used, abused, and manipulated to satisfy your physical cravings? These cravings may be sexual in nature, or psychological as in the form of power or greed.

Our relationships with others must be first filtered through our relationship with Christ. When He is our love, our life, and our Lord, we will have a right mindset about others. We will see everyone as image-bearers of God, potential in His capable hands. As we grow in Christ, we will no longer need the approval of people to make us feel better about ourselves. Instead, we will be satisfied in our identity in Christ.

assignment ....

Evaluate your current relationships. Ask God to show you any areas of abuse.

day 5 **FOURTH LAYER: PAST HURTS**

Finally, we are making it to the top level of our wound and by God's grace we are healing nicely. The top layer of the wound to be healed is past hurts. Read Jeremiah 9:7-11. Who is the person in mourning? For what reason does He weep and wail?

God understands what must happen; yet He weeps over the reality. In your own life, God will allow you to feel the pain of consequences so that you will move out of bad circumstances. As we are enduring those consequences, though, it is appropriate to mourn. Mourning can be a good thing. If we want to be healed from past hurts, we must properly grieve through them. More will be said about the grieving process in Lesson 9. For now, however, let's evaluate how we have handled past hurts. Are your family relationships weighed down by unresolved past hurts? Consider these three areas:

1. Whom do you need to forgive for hurting you?

2. Do you need to ask forgiveness from someone you have hurt?

3. Do you need to mourn these hurts — those done to you and those done by you? If so, how?

Read Jeremiah 9:7-11 again. Here we see the mystery of God's sovereignty and the sufferings of this world. God is in control of Jerusalem's fate, yet He weeps over what must be done. Perhaps you have had difficulty in reconciling God's goodness with the evil of this world. Though we may never fully understand this mystery, we can rest in knowing that God is in control and He is just and right. At the same time, we remember that we live in a fallen world still affected by sin. One day, with the return of Christ, this world will be set right and everything shall be restored and made perfect. In the present time, we are encouraged to remember that God sees our hurts, and He has compassion on us. He will not waste one ounce of our pain and suffering, but instead will work it for our good (Romans 8:28).

assignment ....

In light of today's lesson, reflect on the complete Serenity Prayer:

God, give us grace to accept with serenity

the things that cannot be changed,

Courage to change the things

which should be changed,

and the wisdom to distinguish

the one from the other.

Living one day at a time,

Enjoying one moment at a time,

Accepting hardship as a pathway to peace,

Taking, as Jesus did,

This sinful world as it is,

Not as I would have it,

Trusting that You will make all things right,

If I surrender to Your will,

So that I may be reasonably happy in this life,

And supremely happy with You forever in the next.

Amen.[2]

---

2. Reinhold Niebuhr, "Serenity Prayer," *The Essential Reinhold Niebuhr: Selected Essays and Addresses* (New Haven, CT: Yale UniversityPress, 1983), p. 251.

memory verse review .... Lessons 1–5

LESSON 1 — *I press on toward the goal for the prize of the upward call of God in Christ Jesus. (Philippians 3:14)*

LESSON 2 — *"For I know the plans I have for you," declares the LORD, "plans for welfare and not for evil, to give you a future and a hope." (Jeremiah 29:11)*

LESSON 3 — *Let no corrupting talk come out of your mouths, but only such as is good for building up, as fits the occasion, that it may give grace to those who hear. (Ephesians 4:29)*

LESSON 4 — *Submitting to one another out of reverence for Christ. (Ephesians 5:21)*

LESSON 5 — *For from the least to the greatest of them, everyone is greedy for unjust gain; and from prophet to priest, everyone deals falsely. They have healed the wound of My people lightly, saying, "Peace, peace," when there is no peace. (Jeremiah 6:13-14)*

lesson 6 *summary*

JEREMIAH'S WORLD — FAKE PEACE

The prophets and priests were proclaiming, "Peace! Peace!" But there was no peace. They told the people what they wanted to hear and avoided dealing with the real issues.

APPLICATION

Healthy families realize that peace cannot be manufactured or faked. Real peace comes from God. When we are walking in harmony with God, submitted to His will and His ways, we feel the fullness of His presence and we enjoy peace in that presence.

lesson

6

SHALOM IN THE HOME

memory verse

May the LORD give strength to His people! May the LORD bless His people with peace! (Psalm 29:11)

day 1   SHALOM IS DEFINED AS
SEEING GOD'S FACE

This week we will finish up with Jeremiah 6:13-15. The prophets and priests treat the wounds as if they are no big deal, saying, "peace, peace" when there is no peace. We want to focus in on that word *peace*. You will likely recognize the original word from which we translate peace — *shalom*. This is a special word that actually characterizes a mindset in Hebrew thought. First, let's define the word.

Shalom — the general meaning behind the root is completion and fulfillment — of entering a state of wholeness and unity: peace, completeness, wholeness, harmony/balance. This sort of peace has its source in God.

Here are some Old Testament passages that utilize the word *shalom* (emphasis added).

*Let me hear what God the LORD will speak, for He will speak **peace** to His people, to His saints; but let them not turn back to folly. (Psalm 85:8)*

*May the LORD give strength to His people! May the LORD bless His people with **peace**! (Psalm 29:11)*

*The LORD bless you and keep you; the LORD make His face to shine upon you and be gracious to you; the LORD lift up His countenance upon you and give you **peace**. (Numbers 6:24-26)*

In the priestly prayer in Numbers 6:24-26, what repeated words do you notice?

The Hebrew word for *face* is *panim*. This same word also can be translated as "presence." The idea of God's face turned toward you illustrates you being in His presence. Imagine that you walk into a room and a person is already in the room with his back turned away from you. You don't really feel like you are in his presence until he turns around and sees you. This prayer celebrates God's face turned toward us. In other words, the priest prays that the people will dwell in God's presence and walk in a way that invites His full presence in their lives. Actually, God is omnipresent, meaning there is nowhere that He is not (Psalm 139:7-10). We are never really out of His presence. He never turns His back to us. Maybe we would like Him to turn away from us when we know we are not acting as we should! But He never will.

This prayer in Numbers 6 implies that the people should live in such a way that they would not hinder God's presence and activity in their lives. God's presence brings shalom in our lives. When we choose to live in rebellion to God, does His presence leave us? Not at all. The presence that should bring peace, however, now brings conviction. When we are walking in harmony with God, submitted to His will and His ways, we feel the fullness of His presence and we enjoy peace in that presence.

assignment

Reflect on the concept of God's face turned toward you. He sees you. Does this thought bring peace or conviction? Explain your answer.

day 2   SHALOM IS NOT
                   THE ABSENCE OF
                   TURMOIL/CONFLICT

Shalom comes from God's presence; it is a blessing and gift from God.

Today in Israel, shalom is used as a greeting, both as a hello and goodbye. As a matter of fact, it is the equivalent to the English greeting "How are you doing?" It goes something like this in Hebrew: "Is there any peace for/in you?" Imagine greeting each other in this pointed way. Well, is there any peace in you? Describe where you are right now in your walk with the Lord. Is there peace? If not, why not?

In order for us to truly understand what shalom is, we first need to identify what it is not.

A concept from last week's lesson is that we can't ignore the wounds. We must seek health through and through. Therefore, avoiding conflict altogether is not the way to get peace. Was there a peacekeeper in your family? These people won't allow any disagreements or conflict at all costs. While you may have peace on the surface level, the relationships really are not healthy because issues are not being resolved. Amazingly, families can live together with serious dysfunction and no one will bring it up for decades! Does your family have the proverbial/well-known elephant in the room that no one will mention for the sake of peace?

We learned also that we must be willing to do those healthy self-inspections to make sure we are not the problem, including the communication tips discussed in an earlier lesson. True peace will come only when that wound has been healed thoroughly. Are you willing to have some difficult conversations?

Make a list of situations that need to be dealt with in order for your family to have real peace.

day 3   SHALOM IS NOT THE ABSENCE OF OFFENSE

Perhaps you hesitate to start some healing conversations because you know the person on the receiving end has a short fuse. Peeling off the bandage to treat the wound would only set the person off into a rage. How are you to respond to this?

Similarly, do you have abusive people in your life that always seem to suck you into their dysfunction? Your love for this person causes you to keep going back, yet you know it will cost you in many ways.

For both of these situations, part of finding peace is learning how to set healthy boundaries. In other words, your move toward healthiness may offend people. For the rageaholics, your probing of the wound will make them angry. They will interpret your actions as a personal attack. With those who drag you down into their messy lives, they will be offended at what may seem like your betrayal because you refuse to be part of unhealthy situations. Shalom is not the absence of offense. Yes, your move to a healthy relationship may offend people. The gospel message itself brought offense. Jesus said to expect that the truth would offend some people and cause division. Read Matthew 10:34-39 and Luke 12:51-53 and give a summary below.

Truth brings division sometimes. When we are talking about families, we don't want to end here at the point of division. We pray that the division is temporary and a step on the journey to wholeness. How do you respond when the truth you bring to an unhealthy relationship causes that person to be angry with you or offended and hurt by you?

You must learn how to set healthy boundaries with people. Their mess, or their anger, or their hurt feelings should not dictate your peace. A healthy boundary says, "I still love you completely, but I will not let you pull my emotional strings. I will not let you rob my joy. I will not mirror the anger or unhealthy response you are expressing to me." You have control of yourself and your emotions, not anyone else's. You can't make yourself responsible for their behavior or their reaction to truth.

While it is true that you may need to speak pointedly into a difficult and explosive situation, you should always do so in love. A good rule of thumb is to question yourself first: "What is my motive for speaking truth to this person?" If the answer is to bring about healing and growth in yourself and the person, then speak. If the answer is to help the person be better, then speak.

If the answer is to put the person in his or her place, to set them straight and show them they can't get anything over on you, then don't speak! Until your motive is love, hold your tongue.

assignment ....

Evaluate yourself concerning your current relationships. Do you love people with a healthy boundary, or do their reactions control your actions and feelings? Do you speak the truth in love?

day 1   **SHALOM IS NOT THE ABSENCE OF TROUBLE**

Shalom in your life does not mean the absence of trouble. Read John 16:33 and give a summary below.

In this world we will have trouble (tribulation). Don't wait for some magic day to come when we enjoy trouble-free lives. Even though we work to make our relationships healthy, we will still experience some form of trouble on a regular basis. Jesus promises us that He gives peace even in this troubled world. Read the passages below and see how we experience peace in our lives despite our circumstances.

Shalom is:

1. Peace available through Jesus Christ — John 14:25-27

2. A fruit of the Spirit — Galatians 5:22-23

3. A position before God — Romans 5:1

4. Able to be spread to others — Luke 10:5-7

As we stated previously, *shalom* is a Hebrew term and was part of the mentality of the Old Testament people of God. In the New Testament, we see a specific greeting that appears to be created just for Christians. "Grace and peace to you" occurs in almost every epistle in the New Testament. Paul coined a new term that linked the shalom of God to the grace of God offered in Christ Jesus. The bottom line is this: You want peace? Seek Jesus. Follow Jesus. Be filled with His Spirit and He will direct you as you work toward healthy relationships with others.

assignment

In what ways have you sought peace in your life? According to the Scriptures in today's lesson, who or what provides peace?

day 5   **SHALOM STRENGTHENED IN OUR LIVES**

In order to make sure you have a clear understanding of the material covered this week, provide a brief answer for the questions that follow:

How would you describe the concept of shalom?

Give three examples of what shalom is not.

assignment ....

How do you experience shalom in your life?

Review your memory verse for this week — Psalm 29:11.
See if you can write it below from memory.

HANNAH'S GIFT PLEDGE

As a **Hannah's Gift** *mom, I acknowledge that my children are a gift from God. I take hold of the call and responsibility as a mother and I seek God's guidance on how to best parent my child. I am growing into a wise and strong woman of faith, and my greatest desire is to leave behind a spiritual legacy carried on by my children to their children. May my family prove to be a tower of strength built on the firm foundation I am laying in the power of Christ.*

lesson 7 *summary*

JEREMIAH'S WORLD — TOXIC FAMILY

Jeremiah needed rescuing from the very people he should have been able to trust.

APPLICATION

We must recognize the toxic people in our lives and act appropriately to ensure that they will not endanger us any longer.

lesson

7

TOXIC FAMILIES

memory verses

When I thought, "My foot slips," Your steadfast love, O LORD, held me up. When the cares of my heart are many, Your consolations cheer my soul. (Psalm 94:18-19)

day 1 **HEALTHY BOUNDARIES**
FOR THE RECONCILIATION
OF FAMILIES

The goal of this Bible study, coupled with the first Hannah's Gift™ study, is to equip you to be a godly mother who passes on a spiritual legacy to her family. God loves families. He intended to work in and through family structures to bring about His kingdom work (Deuteronomy 6:4-9, Malachi 4:5-6). As a mother, you are called to take up the responsibility for your own discipleship and the discipleship of your children. Your duty toward your children under your care must be unconditional. Your love for them is unwavering. It does not fade when they fail or disappoint you. You encourage them and build them up and do everything in your power to make them better people. You are entrusted with those children. Our weekly pledge reminds us of the call to godly motherhood.

We have a different responsibility to our other family members, those in our family of origin (our family from our background), even our spouse, in-laws, etc. Last week's lesson taught us how to work toward healthy relationships by speaking truth when needed and setting healthy boundaries with others. We mentioned dysfunctional people who tend to suck us into their messy lives. Sometimes these problems can be remedied as wounds are healed and the parties learn to communicate and relate to each other in healthy ways.

The goal, of course, is reconciliation of families. Sometimes, however, the situation is too toxic to be remedied.

assignment

Begin evaluating your current family relationships. Are there some situations that appear to be beyond remedy?

day 2   **HEALTHY BOUNDARIES**
FROM TOXIC FAMILY MEMBERS

Read about a toxic situation in Jeremiah's life found in Jeremiah 11:18-23. Below is a summary of the main characters:

Jeremiah — prophet, delivering a harsh word from God that is not well received by the people

Men of Anathoth — plotting to kill Jeremiah in order to shut him up

God — coming to Jeremiah's defense just as He promised He would (Jeremiah 1:17-19)

The men of Anathoth were seeking Jeremiah's life. Write the reason why they wanted to kill him as found in Jeremiah 11:19b, 21.

At first glance, this attack on Jeremiah may not surprise you. God had already warned him that the people would hate him and his message. They would try to kill Jeremiah, but God would offer protection to Jeremiah as long as he continued in obedience.

The dramatic twist to this story comes when you fully understand the identity of the men of Anathoth. Go back and read the first verse of the book of Jeremiah (1:1). Where was he from? Who are his people?

That's right. Jeremiah's own family wanted him dead. They plotted to kill him, hoping to catch him off guard since his defenses would likely be down with his own family. Read Jeremiah 11:18-19 again. How did Jeremiah avoid his death? What do you think he meant by *a gentle lamb led to the slaughter*?

assignment . . . .

Have you been endangered by your own family members? Make a list of potential toxic people in your family.

day 3   HEALTHY BOUNDARIES
            WITHIN GOD'S PLAN —
            FAMILY

I pray that not many of you have known an experience like Jeremiah's. My work in the prison, however, tells me that some of you do know the bitter betrayal by your own family members. If you feel comfortable to do so, describe your situation below.

The home setting is supposed to be a representation of the faithfulness of God. Just as God loves us unconditionally, offering us unlimited comfort and support, doing all that is possible to bring us to fullness and completion, so our homes should reflect these same characteristics.

What is one to do if her family of origin is the toxic source that led to, or encouraged, the actions that brought about incarceration?

For example, will you be released from jail to an abusive husband? Is your "support" environment filled with drinkers, users, and pushers? Are there family members out there just waiting for you to be released so that you can join them once again in a life of crime? Simply put, can you trust your family to act in your best interest?

assignment ....

Read Jeremiah 12:6. Honestly evaluate the setting to which you will return upon release from prison. Will you be surrounded by people who will act in your best interest?

day 1   HEALTHY BOUNDARIES BY SEEKING GOD'S HEALING

After yesterday's evaluation, have you become aware of certain family members you need to avoid for your own well-being? How will you respond? You may need to remove yourself and your children from these toxic environments. Think of it as a rescue mission. God had to rescue Jeremiah out of the hands of his family. Review Jeremiah 11:19 again. Has God revealed to you the dangers in your own family? Has He shown you the plots against you from which you must remove yourself?

As if his family trying to kill him isn't bad enough, notice to what class of people Jeremiah's family belonged. See Jeremiah 1:1 and write the response below:

Jeremiah was from the line of priests. He should have been able to trust them to speak the word of the Lord to him. Instead, they acted against God's Word, even to the point of wanting to kill their own flesh and blood. God was faithful to alert Jeremiah (Jeremiah 12:6). In the same way, God will alert you to the dangers within your family. You, then, are responsible to obey what He is telling you to do about it.

You may be wondering how Jeremiah responded to this attack on his life by his family members. Read his complaint to the Lord in Chapter 12:1-4.

Jeremiah experienced betrayal on many levels. His family turned on him. His friends did as well. Read another complaint of his in Jeremiah 20:7-13 and give a summary below:

No wonder we call Jeremiah the Weeping Prophet! What a hard life he had! The ultimate point of despair is recorded in Jeremiah 20:14-18. Read these sad verses now and reflect on the lowest points in your own life. Have you ever been to the point you wished you had never been born?

The Bible gives us many examples of God's people crying out to Him in their despair. You don't have to push down the pain. Speak it to the Lord. The prophet Jeremiah gives you permission. So do many of the Psalms. When we bring our pain to God honestly, He can bring healing and hope out of the darkest circumstances. Keep talking! Keep praying!

assignment

Spend some time reflecting on the family environment waiting for you on the outside. Pray and ask God to give you wisdom on how best to interact with your family. Write below what you sense Him leading you to do.

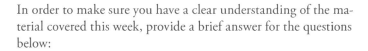

day 5   HEALTHY BOUNDARIES
         IN DISCERNING
         GOD'S DIRECTION

In order to make sure you have a clear understanding of the material covered this week, provide a brief answer for the questions below:

Describe Jeremiah's relationship with his family.

What seemed to be the source of the problem with Jeremiah and his family and friends?

assignment ....

Take a moment to review the answers you gave to the questions in your assignments of the first four days of this week. Do you notice a theme in them that may indicate the direction God is leading you to take? Write down any fears or concerns you have about tackling family-relationship issues.

James 5:16 tells us to confess our sins to one another and pray for one another so that we may be healed. Take time now to confess the part you have played that may have contributed to unhealthy family dynamics.

Review your memory verses — Psalm 94:18-19. See if you can write them below from memory.

lesson **8** *summary*

JEREMIAH'S WORLD — FAMILY SHEPHERDS

Those given the responsibility to shepherd the people had failed. Instead, they withheld life-giving truth from the people, which led to the destruction of the nation.

APPLICATION

Fathers are called to shepherd their families. They are responsible and will give an account to God for the spiritual condition of their family members.

lesson

8

SHEPHERDS AFTER GOD'S HEART

---

memory verses

For you know how, like a father with his children, we exhorted each one of you and encouraged you and charged you to walk in a manner worthy of God, who calls you into His own kingdom and glory. (1 Thessalonians 2:11-12)

day 1   GOD'S DESIGN FOR FAMILY LEADERSHIP

Does the prophet Jeremiah have anything to say about specific family dynamics? Indirectly, yes. To get the clear biblical layout of a healthy family model, read Deuteronomy 6:4-9 and Ephesians 5:22-6:4. Write any responsibilities you see that are directed to parents.

In the Jewish home, the father is seen as the "priest" of his family. A priest should be the representative of God to people and people to God. The family priest is responsible to make sure his children have been taught the truths of God's Word. Discipleship is to be done primarily in the home, not the church. We learned in the first Hannah's Gift study that often men had abused and abandoned their calling to their family and instead victimized the women and children they were supposed to be protecting. This, however, was never how God intended families to be.

assignment

Reflect on Deuteronomy 6:4-9. Write down specific ways you can put these verses into practice now.

day 2   **GOD'S DESIGN**
FOR STRONG MARRIAGES

Today's lesson is found in Ephesians 5:22-6:4. Let's study this Scripture to understand the roles God has established for husbands and wives.

Perhaps the call to submission by a wife to her husband seems out of date to our modern ears. Read Ephesians 5:22-33 again. What comparison is made to the husband/wife relationship?

The idea, then, is a husband loving his wife so much that he would give his life for her. That is the kind of man a wife would not have a problem submitting to, because she knows without a doubt that he has her best interest in mind. Just as Christ gave His all to make us whole and complete, a husband gives his all to present his wife holy and blameless before the Lord.

If you don't mind, I would like to speak frankly about this from a woman's point of view. My husband fulfills this command better than anyone I have ever seen (perhaps I am a bit biased!). He is not threatened at all by my education, my career, or my ministry. He has sacrificed to help me achieve these things. He sincerely desires to see me become all that God has intended for me. And I feel the same way about him. I make sacrifices as well so that he can pursue the calling God has on his life. We mutually submit to one another out of reverence for Christ (Ephesians 5:21). But in the end, he will have to give an account for the spiritual health of our family. He has been assigned as the head for our family. What a responsibility! I want to do all I can to help him succeed in that calling so I encourage him to be the family head. God has wired him with a strong sense of protection and responsibility to provide. You can imagine how important this was in biblical times when a woman didn't have the freedom or opportunity to work and provide for herself and her children. She needed to be under the protection of a loving husband.

In this day and time, it is possible for a woman to make it on her own. She doesn't need the protection of man to survive. However, what do married people tend to produce? Children! The ideal situation, the biblical one, is for children to be raised in an environment of loving parents. Ask any single parent; they will tell you how difficult it is to raise children alone. Sometimes we are forced to do the best we can with our circumstances and God will certainly meet us at the point of our need. A loving, two-parent home, however, is the ideal. With that stated, someone has to raise the children. Kids can raise themselves; we see it all the time. The result, however, is not good. Many of the women in my prison were forced to raise themselves with no positive parental figure in their lives.

assignment ....

Describe your reaction to the husband and wife relationship described in Ephesians 5:22-33. How do past hurts and abuses affect your attitude toward the roles within your family?

Day 3   GOD'S DESIGN FOR SOUND PARENTING

Let's return to the husband as the priest or the responsible head of the home. On his shoulders is placed the responsibility to provide a healthy setting in which the children are to be raised. Someone has to raise the kids. Did I say that already? Yes, someone has to raise the kids. Just as men are typically wired to be protectors and providers, women are wired to be nurturers.

For a time when we were in seminary, my husband did not have a job but was a full-time student while I worked part-time and went to school part-time. He had more time to manage our household and our children's homework schedules and activities. Though he gave it his all and truly put forth a great effort, at the end of the day, nobody can be mama but mama. Those 14 months were difficult for all of us. I wanted to be home with the children because I am better at it. The kids wanted me home too, because I am better at being mom than dad is! Further, my husband was frustrated because he didn't feel that he was fulfilling his role as provider of our home. We both made sacrifices during that time because we felt it was in line with God's plan for our lives. Not only did we make it through that season, but we also learned firsthand about God's design for a mother/wife and a father/husband. This does not mean that a mother cannot have a career. Whether she chooses to work outside the home or not, someone still has to raise the kids. That couple would have to decide how best to provide a nurturing environment for the children in their current situation.

Raising children, however, is just one phase of a woman's life. Now that I am older and I have grown children, I realize how free I am to pursue other ministry responsibilities and career paths that I had to put on hold while my children were little. Why am I telling you all of this? Because we in the 21st century naturally resist a passage like Ephesians 5:22-33. But when we think of the reality of what makes a home healthy, we see the value of what

God asks of husbands and wives. It's not about a husband lording over his wife or getting to be the boss that makes all the decisions. It is about a husband taking seriously his responsibility to see to his family's spiritual, physical, mental, and emotional well-being.

assignment ....

Ephesians 6:1-4 has further guidelines for how to be a godly dad. List the traits you see.

How do children respond to this kind of good parenting?

day 4   **GOD'S DESIGN
FOR FATHERING EXTENDED**

In next week's lesson we will turn to the role of the woman. For now, let's continue our dialogue to men as we learn more about Jeremiah's world. To make the connection fully, we need to make one more side trip to 1 Timothy 3. Read this chapter now and see how a man's role to his family translates to his role over the church. Write any observations below.

Clearly, husbands and fathers who have proven themselves faithful should be church leaders. This standard, however, is expected for all Christian husbands and fathers. The apostle Paul summarizes how every believing man should conduct his activities with his family. The principle is that the man is the shepherd over his family first, and then he may be called to be a shepherd over a flock of God's people. See Paul's comparison of a father as a shepherd in 1 Thessalonians 2:11-12.

You may be saying, "That's great but that is not the spouse I have." Think about these principles:

1. Pray and support the spouse you have to become that kind of man. Forgiveness, communication, and healthy boundaries are essential for this right relationship.

2. Move toward the right kind of parenting yourself. This includes rightly relating to the father of your children.

3. If you have no husband, God has a special place for widows and the fatherless in His love (Psalm 146:9).

4. God calls upon other authorities to establish justice and protection for the fatherless. (Jeremiah 22:3).

assignment

Your memory verses for this week are 1 Thessalonians 2:11-12. Write down some specific characteristics of a godly father.

day 5   **GOD'S DESIGN
IN JEREMIAH'S WORLD**

Now we are ready to return to Jeremiah's world. Clearly, the men
who were to be serving as shepherds over the people were not
doing a very good job. Read the following and make summary
statements about each one:

Jeremiah 5:5-13

Jeremiah 6:13-14

Jeremiah 10:21

Jeremiah 23:1-2

Because the fathers/shepherds have rejected their duty to guard the hearts of the people with truth, what has resulted?

Jeremiah 4:22

Jeremiah 16:10-13

Jeremiah 17:1-2

Notice the common features of the above verses. The children pay the consequences for the sins of the fathers. Because the fathers were not faithful to teach the children about true worship and obedience, the parents and the children will endure the punishment and consequences God warned them about.

What about you? Do you know firsthand what it is like to suffer because of your parents' own neglect of proper living? How about your children? What consequences have they suffered because of your neglect or rejection of God's truth?

Many of us have great regrets when we reflect on the impact our actions have had on our families. Thanks be to God, He does not throw us away or leave us in our despair! In Him, there is always hope of restoration. See the following verses that describe how God plans to correct the situation of poor shepherds. Make summary statements about each one:

Jeremiah 3:14-15

Jeremiah 23:3-8

God is faithful even when we are not. No matter where we are, no matter what mess we have made of our lives, it is never too late to turn to God and give Him the broken pieces. He is a master restorer. He can make faithful shepherds. Jeremiah 23:5 says this hope is grounded in a righteous Branch of David. Who is this person the prophet describes? I will give you a hint. He is the one who made a way for us to be restored back to God and then gave us His Spirit so that we can be faithful shepherds. If you guess Jesus Christ, you are correct! Would you put your faith in Him today and ask Him to have His way in your life?

assignment ....

If you have had unfaithful shepherds in your life, read 1 Peter 1:18-20. Be glad in knowing that, in Christ, you can be redeemed from the empty way of life passed down to you by your earthly fathers.

Review your memory verses — 1 Thessalonians 2:11-12. See if you can write them below from memory.

lesson 9 summary

JEREMIAH'S WORLD — GRIEVING MOTHERS

Jeremiah uses the comparison of weeping mothers to show grief for the ones taken into captivity. The children represent the ones living in exile. The Lord tells Jeremiah that work done through the suffering would be rewarded.

APPLICATION

A mother's compassion for her children reflects God's great compassion for His people. If we cooperate with God's redeeming work while in captivity, He can turn our weeping into rejoicing!

lesson

9

WEEPING MOTHERS WILL REJOICE

---

memory verse

As one whom his mother comforts, so I will comfort you;
you shall be comforted in Jerusalem. (Isaiah 66:13)

day 1 RACHEL AT RAMAH

Last week we looked at the role of the father in the family. This week we turn our attention to the mother. Let us begin with Jeremiah 31:15-20. Read carefully and write down what you think it means.

To fully understand these verses, you must first realize what the place of Ramah and the person Rachel represent. This passage is poetic. It uses symbolism to make a bold statement.

The place Ramah is the city just north of Jerusalem where the exiles were gathered before being deported to Babylon. The picture is of a mother weeping uncontrollably as she watches her child being taken away from her.

The woman Rachel is symbolic for the mother in Judah. Jacob, the father of the 12 sons who become the leaders of the 12 tribes of Israel, was married to Rachel. By using the mother of the 12 tribes, Jeremiah relays two images in one.[3] First, Rachel symbolically represents a mother who has lost her children, the entire nation, to exile. Second, Rachel represents the countless weeping mothers who literally lost their children by death or through captivity by the Babylonians.

Now that you have an idea of the event this Scripture symbolizes, read the verses again. What do you think is meant by the statement *she refuses to be comforted*?

---

3. Rachel was the mother of Joseph and Benjamin and the grandmother of Ephraim and Manasseh. This connected her to both the northern and southern regions, thus making her an appropriate mother figure of all the tribes.

assignment ·

Have you ever had a loss so great that for a time you refused to be comforted? If not, have you ever witnessed someone else exhibit a resistance to being comforted in his or her time of grief?

day 2   GROWTH THROUGH GRIEVING

In Lesson 5 we discussed the need to grieve our losses. Let's unpack this a bit more now. Our Western mindset does not place an importance on grieving. We tend to be uncomfortable with those dealing with loss. Further, we tend to associate mourning with weakness. Indeed, we are weak and helpless when we mourn. The pain of loss cripples us and pushes us past the point of our mental and emotional stability. Seeing others in this state makes us uncomfortable and truthfully, we want people to get over it quickly and return to a state of normalcy.

While this tendency to avoid grief may be status quo in America, this is not the biblical model for handling loss. The Hebrew mindset of the Old Testament understood that grief is a normal part of life and must be dealt with in a healthy manner. Read Ecclesiastes 3:1-8. What does this passage say about loss?

We must face our grief and loss and continue to dialogue with God until we are no longer entangled by it. This doesn't mean that we let go of the memories of the person, position, or thing that we have lost, but rather we are able to move those memories to a proper place in our lives as we go on into our future.

assignment ....

Describe your reaction to Ecclesiastes 3:1-8. Do these verses cause you to feel peace or frustration? Are you hanging on to grief in a way that prohibits you from moving into your future?

day 3   **REWARD IN OUR REPENTANCE**

For Jeremiah's audience, Rachel represented all the women who had lost their children to exile or death because of the war with the Babylonians. How does her grief relate to our lives today? How does it relate specifically to the incarcerated setting?

The hardest part of my job as a prison chaplain is the giving of death notices. The absolute worst is to tell a mother that her child is dead. That is a grief no amount of comforting can touch. For a season, that mother must refuse to be comforted because the crushing pain is too personal; she is unable to let anyone else in. Almost certainly that mother will cry out, "Oh, I wish it could have been me instead!"

Not long after I started working for the prison, I was called to give a grief notice of a different kind. An inmate, who was serving a very long sentence herself, had to be told that her 21-year-old son had just been arrested for first-degree murder. As you can imagine, all kinds of sorrow welled up and spilled over. She cried out over her own mistakes that took her out of her son's life. She blamed herself for his fate. She wept as a mother who had just lost her son to death. She grieved over her own son's future life in prison.

When faced with such loss, we must allow ourselves to grieve. We need to take as long as is needed to weep and wail. But the day will come when we must turn and let the healing begin. Read Jeremiah 31:15-17 again.

What do you think is meant by the statement in verse 16 ... *for there is a reward for your work* ... ?

In Jeremiah's context, this picture shows the people who have gone into captivity as the lost children, and the ones who stayed behind as the weeping mother. When applied to the situation of the incarcerated mother, she can identify with both the mother separated from her child and the symbolic children who were taken to captivity. The name Ephraim is the name of one of Rachel's grandchildren. When that name is used in verses 18-20, it refers to the ones in captivity.

assignment ·

The bottom line is that there is work to be done while incarcerated. And that work will be rewarded. So mother, grieve your losses. Admit your role in your current situation and repent. Read Jeremiah 31:17-19 to help you verbalize this. Write your response below:

day 4   **GOD IN OUR GRIEF**

God doesn't leave you in the dust of sorrow. He will restore you if you will let Him have His way in your life. Read Jeremiah 31:20. Who is speaking? Remember, whom does Ephraim represent? Write your answers below:

God says He yearns for those who were taken into captivity and He longs to return them to the land. God is speaking in verse 20 about His child Ephraim. In other words, as the mothers weep over their lost children, God weeps over His lost children.

He says He ... *will surely have mercy* [compassion] *on him* ... He has mercy (compassion) for you. The word used here for mercy is related to the Hebrew word for a mother's womb. In other words, this kind of mercy is best understood as a mother's love for her child.

Would you agree that there is a unique bond between a mother and child that is unlike any other bonds?

The love and longing you have for your child comes from being made in God's image. God loves and longs for His children. Can you understand that He longs for you to return to Him and be in fellowship with Him even more than you long for your own children?

Dear mothers, we are wired to have mercy (compassion) for our children. That unconditional love comes from our heavenly Father. We can trust Him with our pain and grieving over our children, because He has mourned and grieved over His own children. We want to love our children properly. We want to parent them appropriately, in a way that will result in their good. As we return to Him and let Him discipline and train us during our captivity, He can restore us to proper fellowship with Him and with others.

assignment

Are you willing to let God create in you a mother's love that mirrors His love for His children? How will you make yourself available to God so that He can do a transforming work in you? How can you communicate the love of Christ in providing salvation to your children?

day 5

EXPECTATIONS OF
OUR RESPONSIBILITY

In order to make sure you have a clear understanding of the material covered this week, provide a brief answer for the questions below:

From what city were the exiles gathered up and then taken into captivity?

What was the name of the woman who represented the grieving mothers? Who was she historically?

Whom did the lost children represent?

assignment ·

List five responsibilities you would consider to be expected of every mother.

Now number those five responsibilities in order of importance.

In addition to providing for my basic needs, my mother played an important part in shaping my values, attitudes, and beliefs. Her influence over me cannot be overstated. Because of this I am keenly aware of my role in the lives of my own children. Above all, I want to point them toward Jesus for life and peace and redemption. We can't wait until we have it all figured out. How can you begin today to reflect God's perfect love to your children?

Review your memory verse — Isaiah 66:13. See if you can write it below from memory.

HANNAH'S GIFT PLEDGE

As a **Hannah's Gift** mom, I acknowledge that my children are a gift from God. I take hold of the call and responsibility as a mother and I seek God's guidance on how to best parent my child. I am growing into a wise and strong woman of faith, and my greatest desire is to leave behind a spiritual legacy carried on by my children to their children. May my family prove to be a tower of strength built on the firm foundation I am laying in the power of Christ.

lesson 10 summary

JEREMIAH'S PROMISE OF A NEW COVENANT

Israel had broken their covenant with God, but God remained faithful to them. A new covenant would come which would provide greater access to God and a fuller knowledge of His presence.

APPLICATION

This new covenant was made available to us through Jesus Christ. Through our faith in Him, we are in a permanent relationship with the God of the universe. He made a way for us to know Him even while we were rebellious and blind. Through Jesus, we can experience healthy restoration with our families and others.

lesson

10

PROMISE OF RESTORATION

memory verse

… I have loved you with an everlasting love; therefore I have continued My faithfulness to you. (Jeremiah 31:3)

day 1 RESTORATION OF HOPE

God told Jeremiah his life would be tough and his ministry would be impossible. People hated him for the truth that he brought to them. Even his own family tried to kill him. He was rejected by everyone but his God. Finally, starting at Chapter 30, he gets to change his sermon from gloom and doom to hope and restoration. Brief hints of hope had been sprinkled in his previous messages, but now he gets to maximize on God's plan of restoration. For four chapters, the tone of the book changes. Read Jeremiah 30:1-11 carefully.

Give a comparison from your world for the following statements:

... I will restore the fortunes [return from captivity] *of My people, Israel and Judah ...* (verse 3). In other words, what is your captivity and restoration?

... I will break his yoke from off your neck, and I will burst your bonds, and foreigners shall no more make a servant of him. But they shall serve the LORD their God ... (verses 8-9) In other words, what are the bonds on you that need to be broken, and who are the ones who have enslaved you?

... for behold, I will save you from far away, and your offspring from the land of their captivity ... (verse 10) In other words, what is your far away place and where are your children?

... but of you I will not make a full end ... (verse 11) In other words, can you give evidence that your destruction has not been complete?

assignment . . . .

At the end of verse 11, God says that He will discipline but only in just measure. What do you think this means? How have you experienced God's discipline in just measure?

day 2 COVENANT OF HOPE

Jeremiah 30:1-11 was written for the people of Judah who were part of God's nation. The promise of restoration was a result of them being in covenant with God. Today we will explore the idea of covenant in the Bible.

The term *covenant* reflects a binding relationship between people or groups of people. In our day, we tend to think of a covenant like a legal contract. This, however, does not reflect the concept of biblical covenant. With legal contracts come loopholes and self-serving clauses. With covenant, however, the participants are dedicated to one another until death alone parts them. Sound familiar? Yes, the marriage covenant is the closest example, and is indeed a biblical covenant.

If I enter into a contract with a business partner, then we have a common interest and shared economic investment. In a marriage, however, the two people don't just have a shared interest in each other, they now are defined as family. In effect, covenant defines kinship.[4]

Before my husband and I married, I had my own family and my own life. He had his own family and his own life. When we married, we became each other's next of kin, and we established a new and separate family unit apart from the ones that we came from before. We became family to each other because of covenant.

Before marriage, we each had our own agendas. Now as a married couple, everything I do affects my husband, and everything he does affects me. Our lives are completely interdependent, whether we like it or not!

In addition, everything I owned became his, and everything he owned became mine. I bet you didn't know that community property was a biblical concept!

---

4. For more information, see Frank M. Cross, *From Epic to Canon: History and Literature in Ancient Israel* (Baltimore: Johns Hopkins University Press, 1998).

Lesson 10

These functions of covenant seen in a healthy marriage reflect the concept of covenant in the Bible. While marriage is an example, it is not the only kind of covenant. In ancient times people understood the seriousness of entering into covenant with someone. Here are some basic elements of a covenant:

1. It was active until the death of the covenant partners.

2. The belongings of each one become property of the other.

3. The enemies, battles, and struggles of one are taken on by the other.

4. Each partner is obligated to each other, to serve the best interest of the other.

When covenants were formed in ancient times, they would often involve an animal sacrifice. The animal would be cut in two parts, and the covenant participants would walk between the pieces of the animal. This act symbolized the until death commitment. For a reference to this, see Jeremiah 34:18.

So what does all this mean? Why is the concept of covenant so important? It is important because this is the way in which God chose to reveal Himself and express His love to mankind. He made a covenant. Look over those elements of covenant again. Imagine the God of the universe wanting to become family with mankind! Imagine that God moves to obligate Himself to His covenant partners! And the enemies of man become the enemies of God. And the possessions of God become available to man! Wow! What a thought! How, exactly, did God enter covenant with man? We will look briefly at the main points.

Genesis 12:1-3 describes God inviting Abraham into a relationship. He makes promises to Abraham that reflect covenant thought. In Genesis 15:8-19, we see that covenant confirmed in a traditional ceremony involving the splitting of animals. Since only God walked through the pieces, God alone is obligating Himself to bring about the terms of the covenant given in Genesis 12:1-3.

In Exodus 19-20, we see this covenant extended to the great nation that came from Abraham's line. Abraham's line becomes the people of God. As a nation, they are in covenant with God. Jeremiah's people living in Judah are of this line. They still see themselves as God's covenant partner. Jeremiah is used by God to tell His covenant partner that they have sinned and will experience judgment. But because He is faithful to His covenant, He will provide a time of restoration.

assignment . . . .

Read and review Jeremiah 30:1-11 again. God isn't going to break off their yokes and save a remnant of Judah just because He decided to be a nice guy. Instead, He is acting in faithfulness to His covenant. Tomorrow we will see how we can be receivers of such loyalty.

day 3   JESUS' BLOOD GIVES HOPE

Does the covenant between God and Abraham's line have anything to do with us today? Stay with me, and I will show you that it does.

Remember reading in Jeremiah the scattered words of hope about one to come from the line of David? We discussed in Lesson 9 that the Righteous One from David's line is Jesus. Jeremiah's people, however, do not know this yet. They only know that they failed as God's covenant partner by neglecting His commands and running after other gods. God has already used divorce language to illustrate how broken the covenant was. Yet here God says they will be His people. How? Surely something must be done about the broken covenant. Read Jeremiah 31:31-32.

Note Jeremiah speaks toward the future. He speaks of a new covenant to be established at some point in the future. God has not thrown away His people (see verse 31), but He has a plan to redefine who His people will be. Read Jeremiah 31:31-34 again, and make a note of the characteristics of God's people under this new covenant.

In other words, being part of Abraham's line will no longer label you as God's people. No longer will an external law determine God's people as seen in Exodus 19-20. See what the prophet Ezekiel had to say about the same situation in Ezekiel 36:24-28 and make notes about the changes of God's people.

Jeremiah has already stated that the hope to come lies in the One to come from the line of David. Link this together by looking at some New Testament verses:

Jesus is of the line of David: See His genealogy (family tree) in Matthew 1:1-17. Jesus is both from the line of Abraham and of David.

Jesus fulfills Jeremiah's new covenant. See Matthew 26:26-28, Mark 14:24-25, and Luke 22:20. These all speak of the same event when Jesus reinterpreted the bread and wine of the Passover event to point to Himself as the sacrifice for the new covenant. Remember the sacrifice that typically was a part of the covenant ceremony? Yes, Jesus is that sacrifice for the new covenant. Then who are the partners of the new covenant? God and every person who has put their faith in Christ as Savior. Go back and read those characteristics of a covenant from Day 2. If you are in Christ, God is your faithful covenant partner! You can take full confidence in knowing every battle you have is now His, and every blessing of heaven He purposely desires for you to enjoy!

The Holy Spirit now identifies those who are God's people (Romans 8:9-17). No longer can the family tree or the written law determine who belongs to God. Since Christ came and brought in the new covenant in His blood, those who have faith in Jesus are given His Spirit and know to whom they belong.

Remember the letter Jeremiah wrote to the ones in exile? He gave them the following promise: *For I know the plans I have for you, declares the LORD, plans for welfare and not for evil, to give you a future and a hope (Jeremiah 29:11).*

The time of restoration Jeremiah describes in Chapters 30-33 is dependent on the people turning back to the Lord. He said He would be found by those who seek Him with their whole heart. We have an opportunity to know God even more intimately than what was available to Jeremiah's people. Since we have Jesus, we have access to God and may approach Him in confidence (Hebrews 4:14-16)! We have the awesome privilege of being filled with His Spirit so that we can walk in His ways (Galatians 5:16-25).

assignment

What does it mean to you to ... *with confidence draw near to the throne of grace ...*? How do you feel about Jesus being able to sympathize with you about temptations? (See Hebrews 4:14-16.)

day 4   HOPE GIVES HEALING

Read the end of the promise portion of Jeremiah in 33:1-16 and answer the questions below:

What offer does God make to His people in verse 3?

What will be the condition of the land in Jeremiah's day (verses 4-5)?

What does God promise to be the future condition of the land and God's people (verses 6-9)?

Make an application of verses 10-11 to your own life.

This promise of restoration is based on the coming of what person (see verses 12-16)?

The hope of our desolate lands becoming places of praise lies with Jesus Christ. Do you see why it is so important that you know Him, and then help your family know Him? Jesus *came to seek and to save the lost (Luke 19:10)*. He came to give life abundantly (John 10:10). He came to restore us back to God by paying the price for our sins (2 Corinthians 5:21).

Quoting from another Old Testament prophet, Jesus said this about His mission: *"The Spirit of the Lord is upon Me, because He has anointed Me to proclaim good news to the poor. He has sent Me to proclaim liberty to the captives and recovering of sight to the blind, to set at liberty those who are oppressed, to proclaim the year of the Lord's favor" (Luke 4:18-19)*.

Jesus is the Great Restorer. Put your hope in Him to restore and rebuild your family. Let His Spirit guide you in the right steps to bring this about. May your family one day praise together: *"… Give thanks to the LORD of hosts, for the LORD is good, for His steadfast love endures forever! …" (Jeremiah 33:11)*.

assignment

Review your memory verse — Jeremiah 31:3. See if you can write it below from memory.

day 5   **MY RESPONSE
TO RESTORATION**

What have you learned during this 10-week study that you want to pass on to your family? Use the following to prompt your responses.

The plans and activities that I need to **stop** thinking about and being involved with are:

The areas of **caution** I need to be more aware about are:

The responses I need to pray about **starting** or **beginning** are:

Adjustments in my present incarceration circumstances …

Positive communication in my relationships with my children, with my family, and with others …

Dealing with the wounds in my family or others…

Paving pathways of peace/shalom for myself…

memory verse review .... Lessons 6–10

LESSON 6 — *May the LORD give strength to His people! May the LORD bless His people with peace! (Psalm 29:11)*

LESSON 7 — *When I thought, "My foot slips," Your steadfast love, O LORD, held me up. When the cares of my heart are many, Your consolations cheer my soul. (Psalm 94:18-19)*

LESSON 8 — *For you know how, like a father with his children, we exhorted each one of you and encouraged you and charged you to walk in a manner worthy of God, who calls you into His own kingdom and glory. (1 Thessalonians 2:11-12)*

LESSON 9 — *As one whom his mother comforts, so I will comfort you; you shall be comforted in Jerusalem. (Isaiah 66:13)*

LESSON 10 — *… I have loved you with an everlasting love; therefore I have continued My faithfulness to you. (Jeremiah 31:3)*

facilitator's notes

REVIEW OF HANNAH'S GIFT

Hannah's Gift and Malachi Dads™ set the tone for parents to assume responsibility for being godly influences and to build a legacy of faith and hope in Christ. As a part of the Awana Lifeline™ ministry, these programs focus on becoming strong believers in Christ who will then be able to impact their own families and indeed other families. As faith in Christ changes the inmate, they in turn can be a force for change in their own families.

HANNAH'S GIFT PLEDGE

As a Hannah's Gift mom, I acknowledge that my children are a gift from God. I take hold of the call and responsibility as a mother and I seek God's guidance on how to best parent my child. I am growing into a wise and strong woman of faith, and my greatest desire is to leave behind a spiritual legacy carried on by my children to their children. May my family prove to be a tower of strength built on the firm foundation I am laying in the power of Christ.

OVERVIEW OF *FAMILY RESTORATION*

Building on the growth incarcerated women experienced in *The Heart of a Mother, Family Restoration* goes beyond this by assisting these moms in taking positive steps toward healthy family structures upon release.

PRELIMINARIES

Whether this is a group that has been together for *Hannah's Gift: The Heart of a Mother* or a newly formed group of *The Heart of a Mother* graduates, introduce yourself and have each participant do the same. You will also want to know the names and the ages of each of their children.

You want to generate an atmosphere of prayer for one another. In establishing a system of prayer, have index cards available for each participant on which they can write their prayer needs.(Names on the cards are not necessary.) Make prayer an integral and normal weaving of each lesson — either at the beginning, the closing, or whenever you sense the need. Many of the application questions for discussion pause for a time of prayer response. Make wise use of these cards yourself as you pray and care for the women throughout the week.

Along with a study and questions for five days of each week, the participant is also encouraged to memorize the memory verses found on the summary pages. You may want to create a motivational chart with the participants' names and columns for each verse. When the verse has been recited (or written on an index card from memory), she gets a star or a check in that column.

Allow participants to share a step in their journey of becoming a godly mother and highlights of life change from the first Hannah's Gift study. Listen for the disappointments as well as victories but keep the discussion brief and positive. You may want to share your own growth and struggles as you have helped others during your leading of the previous Hannah's Gift study. This will begin to build a trust with your current group of women.

Note: Some of you may want to have an introductory session before beginning the 10 weeks of study (making it an 11 week study). This would include getting acquainted with each member, introducing the prayer index cards, and sharing reflections from the *Hannah's Gift: The Heart of a Mother* study along with giving the *Family Restoration* books to the women. You will want to communicate the expectations for lesson study, memorization of verses, and review of the Hannah's Gift Pledge.

Others of you will have distributed the books prior to the first week so the participants have completed Lesson 1 and are ready for the discussion with the group. The above paragraphs are necessary, though, at the beginning. Introductions and sharing will need to be included but brief so that Lesson 1 discussion happens.

FACILITATING A SMALL GROUP

Remember that each participant's situation is unique. Some may have no visits from their children; some may have a very poor relationship with the child's caregiver. Not everyone will end the program at the same place. Your responsibility is to help move each mom toward restoration with her family relationships. Resist the temptation to tell her what to do to get the results she desires. Keep an open dialogue so that she can come to the right conclusions herself. Keep praying and pointing toward the truth of Scripture as you trust in the work of the Holy Spirit.

Ideally, a small group is best with five to seven participants with no more than 10 for one facilitator. The following notes should give you the instructions you need to have a productive small group experience. Included is a description of the types of discussion questions; a big idea for each week and knowledge, understanding and application questions for the lessons.

DISCUSSION QUESTIONS

These are the types of questions that shape your discussion for your small groups:

Knowledge

- The response is usually found in Scripture or in the writing of the book.
- The question helps participants to observe facts, principles, and information.
- The answer will review, "What does the Bible say or what does this book say?"

Understanding

- The response looks at what it means to life and the culture in general.
- The question will begin to draw out the meaning and wisdom of this study.
- The answer will be firmly based in the Word, but guide to the question, "What does it mean?"

APPLICATION

- The response flows to specific uses of the insights that the Bible and this book have given the participant.

- The question will prompt life change and faith commitments.

- The answer will lead to specific steps of obedience to the Lord answering, "What does this mean to me?"

In your leading and guiding of this study, questions can be processed either by:

1. Answering each question as it presents itself in the text for each week

2. Looking at the knowledge-understanding-application questions within each section of the study

3. Having the knowledge-understanding-application questions guide a smooth transition from general information to understanding and wisdom to specific obedience

The subsequent discussion notes will follow the third process. With these questions, one does not need to ask all of the questions but ask at least one good discussion question within each type and continue to guide and allow for more answers with connecting questions (i.e., "Good, what else do you see or observe?", "OK, others?", "Any other comments?", "Anyone have more insight?"). Be careful that the most important questions are discussed.

Lesson 1 ....

Introduction

BIG IDEA

Using Jeremiah's words and warnings as signposts, the participants will be ***introduced*** to the journey of building healthy family structures upon release.

DISCUSSION QUESTIONS

Knowledge

1. Contrast the false prophets' message with Jeremiah's message of judgment from God. (Answers are from Scripture.)

2. How are Jeremiah's times like our own?

Understanding

1. What did you learn about God's relationship to His people?

2. What false worship activities, false securities, false hopes, and false realities do people put their confidence in today?

3. What principles for building healthy families have we learned?

APPLICATION

1. What false worship, false securities, false hopes, and false realities do you want to eliminate from your life? How do you think you should go about doing that?

2. What are you (can you be) praying for now as you build healthy relationships beyond your captivity to leave a spiritual legacy for your family?

The Years of Captivity

BIG IDEA

To strengthen their relationships with their children and other family members, the women will be challenged to learn and practice during their **captive years.**

DISCUSSION QUESTIONS

Knowledge

1. What are the parts of God's promise as described in Jeremiah 29:11-14? What does God do? What are the people to do?

2. What were some of the plans (false prophet's message and people's vain hopes) that went astray as we learned this week?

Understanding

1. In what ways does an incarceration facility compare to the captivity of Jeremiah's day (See chart from Day 4.)?

2. What plans do you see people making for themselves when they refuse to trust God?

APPLICATION

1. In memorizing Jeremiah 29:11, what actions of verses 12-14 need the most focus and strengthening in your own life?

2. What aspects of settling in are difficult for you? What advice and prayer do you need from others?

lesson 3

Settling in: Healthy Communication

BIG IDEA

Healthy communication skills will be emphasized for the inmates to apply during and after incarceration.

DISCUSSION QUESTIONS

Knowledge

1. Which of the Scriptures that you read and studied this week provided the strongest communication principles, in your view?

2. Which of the three communication questions asked in Day 2 are the most important to you?

Understanding

1. Have you seen tough times get turned into healthy relationship opportunities?

2. What do you think is the difference between sharing prayer concerns and gossip?

APPLICATION

1. Which communication tip needs to be applied to your life this next week?

2. What can you do to strengthen communication with your family using the principles from this lesson's study?

Lesson 4

Settling in: Submit to Authority

BIG IDEA

The Christian characteristic of an attitude of *submission* will be examined.

DISCUSSION QUESTIONS

Knowledge

1. Summarize the biblical teaching about the place of authority in a believer's life. What are the correct responses to authority according to the Bible?

2. What is the contrast that the Bible describes between Jeremiah's response to authority and the people's responsibility to God's message?

Understanding

1. Share some current day examples of the key points listed from Day 4.

2. What are possible present day cisterns that keep people from trusting in the living water of God?

APPLICATION

1. What patterns of life that reflect the environment (Day 4) need to change in your life?

2. Have you come to a place of submitting to Christ:
   a. By believing in Him for your salvation?
   b. By trusting Him for your ability to live in your circumstances?
   c. By extending this trust to His work in your family?

Lesson 5

Treat the Wounds

BIG IDEA

Honesty will be key as the members *treat their wounds* for deep healing.

DISCUSSION QUESTIONS

Knowledge

1. Define each layer of the wounds that needs to be healed as described in the lesson.

2. Review the message of 1 John 1:8-2:2. What specific steps are believers called to do and what specific steps does God do?

Understanding

1. What is the outcome of not healing a wound completely? Do you see similar results in the lives of others; i.e., families, friends, countries?

2. Look again at Galatians 5:22-23. Apply each part of the fruit of the Spirit to a specific problem in families today. What would be different if families would function according to each of these?

APPLICATION

1. Examine again the three questions about past, unresolved family hurts from Day 5. What is the Holy Spirit prompting you to ask in regard to these questions?

2. What spiritual surgeries need to happen in your life to assure that you are completely healed?

3. Review and say the Serenity Prayer together.

Lesson 6

Shalom in the Home

BIG IDEA

Understanding how ***shalom***/peace can be strengthened and enjoyed will be the focus.

DISCUSSION QUESTIONS

Knowledge

1. Have each person choose a verse about shalom/peace and share it with the group. (This will enable important verses to be reviewed for later discussion.)

2. What does shalom *not* mean?

Understanding

1. Where does the resource for living in shalom come from?

2. How well is shalom understood in your life, your present living circumstances, or your family on the outside?

APPLICATION

1. What are some areas of your life that might cause God to look away (Isaiah 59:1-2)? Remind the group of 1 John 1:8-2:2 as they continue the deep healing of God's forgiveness for their lives.

2. Look again at Numbers 6:22-26. Can you pray a similar prayer for your family? What would it say?

Toxic Families

BIG IDEA

Recognizing the healthy boundaries from ***toxic people*** will be crucial to tackling the fears and concerns of relationship issues.

DISCUSSION QUESTIONS

Knowledge

1. What are the characteristics of the toxic people in Jeremiah's life?

2. What present-day toxic people are described in this lesson?

Understanding

1. What impact do toxic people have on a believer's life or family functioning? Using the list from the previous questions, which of these characteristics most likely show up in our lives?

2. How would you describe God's plan for families to be demonstrated today? (Check Deuteronomy 6:4-9.)

APPLICATION

1. What causes you to be a weeping prophet like Jeremiah? Prompt some of the concerns that we have for our families. Have the participants choose one or two events, attitudes, or dangers about which they need prayer and allow the group to pray for each other.

2. What change in communication needs to be established in your life for a healthy boundary?

Shepherd's After God's Heart

BIG IDEA

God's heart for family and the roles within it will be studied.

DISCUSSION QUESTIONS

Knowledge

1. What are the roles God has established for husbands and wives?

2. What is the impact on children of good and bad parenting?

Understanding

1. Develop practical suggestions for a Deuteronomy 6 Practical Parenting Checklist. Have participants suggest how to love the Lord and have His word on their heart in these settings:
   - In the home (personal — *frontlets* — and public — *write them ... on your gates*)
   - Traveling (*by the way*)
   - Going to bed (*when you lie down*)
   - Morning routine (*when you rise*)

2. What failure in Jeremiah's day has a parallel to today?

APPLICATION

1. Prompt members of the group to pray by name for their children and their caregivers. Encourage them to pray for good fatherly role models — either their children's dads or other Christ-following men.

2. If the group is close, have them share about past hurts from Day 5 and pray for each other.

Lesson 9

Weeping Mothers Will Rejoice

BIG IDEA

The process of grieving or *weeping* will allow for appreciation of God's redeeming work.

DISCUSSION QUESTIONS

Knowledge

1. What do you learn about appropriate grief from this week's lesson?

2. What appointed times or seasons do Ecclesiastes 3:1-8 cause you to think about?

Understanding

1. Trace the cycle of grief which begins with refusing to be comforted and moves to acceptance and trust in Christ. Are these steps obvious to you?

   - Denial and isolation
   - Anger
   - Bargaining
   - Depression
   - Acceptance[5]

2. How do you respond to the idea that Jesus was/is *a man of sorrows, and acquainted with grief ... (Isaiah 53:3)*?

---

5. Elisabeth Kubler-Ross, *On Death and Dying* (New York: Scribner, 1969, 2003).

APPLICATION

1. Gospel presentation — Isaiah 53 is an excellent presentation of the gospel; focus especially on Isaiah 53:4-6 relating to the work of Christ on the cross. If you feel able, you may want to sing a hymn such as *Amazing Grace, When I Survey the Wondrous Cross*, or another sound doctrinal evangelistic tool.

2. Romans 12:15 says: *Rejoice with those who rejoice, weep with those who weep.* Practice this verse as a group in prayer. Begin with "Thanks for that of which we can rejoice," and continue with "We ask for comfort from You for these sorrows."

Lesson 10

Promise of Restoration

BIG IDEA

In this final lesson, the women will respond to **restoration** for their relationships.

DISCUSSION QUESTIONS

Knowledge

1. What are the conditions of a covenant relationship as described in our lesson this week?

2. Trace how Jesus is qualified to be the fulfillment of the new covenant.

Understanding

1. Compare Jeremiah's message to his people with the principles of Hebrews 12:5-11.

2. Why do some today struggle with and reject the covenant relationship offered through Christ?

APPLICATION

1. Ask, "How is your covenant relationship with the Lord Jesus?" Give time for each one in your group to share about their faith in Christ.

2. Day 5 is a review of the spiritual progress and family restoration in the lives of the group participants. Use O-A-T-S to help strengthen each participant's plans for obedience.

- O — Outcome: The goals you want to see happen
- A — Activities: The events and actions which should lead to the outcomes
- T — Time: The timetable of progress with the Lord's help
- S — Systematic Checkup: The accountability which prompts growth

notes

notes

Also from Awana Lifeline ...

Hannah's Gift: Family Restoration

From the first Hannah's Gift book, incarcerated moms have established the importance of on-going activity in the lives of their children. Moms must now take steps to prepare themselves to build healthy family structures upon release. We want to use the prophet Jeremiah's words and warnings as signposts to lead us along the journey to healthy relationships.

Item 97472

Malachi Dads: The Heart of a Father

The Heart of a Father curriculum provides practical, biblical advice for life, marriage and parenting, showing participants how to become Christ followers and grow in their faith. The *Inmate Challenge DVD*, sold separately, is part of the Malachi Dads curriculum, The Heart of a Father. Make sure you order a copy with your books.

Item 95259

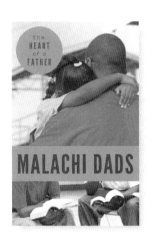

Order today! EMAIL: awanalifeline@awana.org

Malachi Dads: The Heart of a Man, Part 1

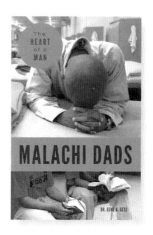

The Heart of a Man, Part 1 is the second book in the Malachi Dads curriculum. This study focuses on how to become a man with a heart that pleases God, no matter what our past sins and failures, and no matter our physical appearance.

Item 97523

Inmate Challenge DVD

Receive a compelling challenge from some of the most broken men in our society — inmate fathers.

Filmed on location at the famed Angola Prison in Louisiana, three inmate fathers share their stories and their challenge to other inmates. This DVD is an ideal launching point for jail or prison ministry and for challenging fathers to consider the legacy they are leaving. Includes a five-week small group discussion guide.

Order along with *Malachi Dads: The Heart of a Father* curriculum. Running time: 45 minutes.

Item 83509

PHONE: **888-944-4292**   WEB: awanalifeline.org/products

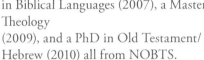

author bio

Kristi Miller is director of an extension center of New Orleans Baptist Theological Seminary located in the Louisiana Correctional Institute for Women, where she also serves as a chaplain. Kristi holds a Master of Divinity with a specialization in Biblical Languages (2007), a Master of Theology
(2009), and a PhD in Old Testament/ Hebrew (2010) all from NOBTS.